Planes

Chris Oxlade

www.heinemann.co.uk
Visit our website to find out more information about Heinemann Library books.

To order:

 Phone 44 (0) 1865 888066

 Send a fax to 44 (0) 1865 314091

 Visit the Heinemann Bookshop at www.heinemann.co.uk to browse our catalogue and order online.

First published in Great Britain by Heinemann Library, Halley Court, Jordan Hill, Oxford OX2 8EJ a division of Reed Educational and Professional Publishing Ltd.
Heinemann is a registered trademark of Reed Educational & Professional Publishing Ltd.

OXFORD MELBOURNE AUCKLAND
JOHANNESBURG BLANTYRE GABORONE
IBADAN PORTSMOUTH (NH) USA CHICAGO

Designed by Paul Davies and Associates
Originated by Ambassador Litho Ltd
Printed in Hong Kong/China

04 03 02 01 00
10 9 8 7 6 5 4 3 2 1

ISBN 0 431 10838 2

British Library Cataloguing in Publication Data

Oxlade, Chris
Planes. – (Transport around the world)
1.Airplanes – Juvenile literature 2.Air travel
– Juvenile literature
I.Title
629.1'3334

Acknowledgements

The Publishers would like to thank the following for permission to reproduce photographs: Corbis: George Hall p21, Vince Streano p25; Photodisc: pp23, 29; Quadrant Picture Library: Jeremy Hoare pp5, 13, R Shaw p7, Flight pp6, 8, 20, 26, p9, p11, Erik Simonsen p12, Trent Jones p15, Mark Wagner p16, LG Photo p17, Anthony R Dalton p18, Paul Phelan p19, Tony Hobbs pp22, 27, p24; The Stock Market: Russell Munson p10; Tony Stone Images: Alan Smith p14, World Perspectives p28; Trip: Malcolm Fife p4

Cover photograph reproduced with permission of Tony Stone

Every effort has been made to contact copyright holders of any material reproduced in this book. Any omissions will be rectified in subsequent printings if notice is given to the Publisher.

Contents

Any words appearing in the text in bold, **like this**, are explained in the glossary.

What is a plane?

A plane is a machine that flies through the air. Some planes carry passengers. Some planes carry **goods** called cargo. People often fly planes for fun.

The person who flies a plane is called the **pilot**. The pilot controls the take-off and landing, and **steers** the plane through the air. Some pilots have computers to help them fly the plane.

How planes work

Wings keep a plane in the air. As the plane flies along, some air rushes under the wings and some air rushes over the wings. The air pushes the wings upwards.

Engines power a plane through the air. This engine makes a **propeller** spin round. The propeller **blades** push air backwards, which makes the plane go forwards.

propeller

blade

engine

Old planes

This plane was called *Flyer 1*. It was the first plane to fly using an **engine**. It was built in 1903 by two American brothers called Orville and Wilbur Wright.

An **airliner** is a plane that carries passengers. This is what an airliner looked like 80 years ago. It was slow and very noisy. This plane has two sets of wings.

Where are planes used?

All planes fly in the air. On long flights, **jet airliners** fly about ten kilometres above the ground. Some smaller planes fly closer to the ground.

You catch a plane at an airport. This is a
busy place with many planes taking off
and landing. Planes take off and land
on a **runway**.

Airliners

Passenger planes are called **airliners**. The Boeing 747 is the biggest airliner in the world. It is sometimes called the jumbo jet.

More than 500 people can sit inside a jumbo jet. During the flight the passengers eat a meal and can watch a film. Jumbo jets fly on long journeys all over the world.

Supersonic planes

Supersonic planes fly through the air faster than sound. Sound speeds along at 1250 kilometres per hour. Supersonic planes go faster than this! Concorde is a supersonic **airliner**.

Concorde has a long, pointed nose.
When Concorde comes in to land, the
nose drops down so that the pilot can
see the **runway** ahead.

Cargo planes

Start

A cargo plane is a plane that carries **goods** or cargo. Inside the plane is a cargo **hold**. During the flight, boxes are tied down to stop them moving about in the hold.

A cargo plane has a huge door that opens wide to let large pieces of cargo into the plane. A special truck lifts the cargo up to the door.

Seaplanes

A seaplane is a plane that takes off and lands on water. Seaplanes are useful in places where there is plenty of water and nowhere to build a **runway**.

Most planes have wheels for landing but a seaplane has two floats instead. The floats let the seaplane skim across the water for take-off and landing.

Vertical take-off

Some planes, such as the Harrier jet, can take off by flying straight up into the air instead of using a **runway**. The Harrier can also fly like a normal plane.

The Harrier has powerful **jet engines**. For take-off and landing, the engine's **nozzles** point downwards. For flying along, they point backwards.

Gliders

A glider is a plane without an **engine**. A glider is towed into the air by another plane and glides slowly back to the ground. People fly gliders for fun.

A glider has long, thin wings. They keep the glider up as it flies slowly along. The glider's smooth shape lets it cut easily through the air.

Microplanes

This tiny plane is called a microlight. It can only carry one or two people. The microlight's wing is made of a plastic sheet fixed to thin metal tubes.

The **pilot's** seat hangs underneath the wing. The pilot **steers** the plane up and down, and to the left and right by moving a bar that is attached to the wing.

Fighting planes

Military planes are used in wars to fight other planes in the air. They also attack targets on the ground. Fighters are small, fast planes that can turn very quickly.

Fighters attack enemy planes with **missiles** and guns. The missiles are fixed under the fighter's wings. To fire a missile, the **pilot** presses a button in the **cockpit**.

ommolow finish

Space planes

The space shuttle is a plane that goes into space. It takes off like a rocket. Booster rockets give it an extra push.

parachute

When its job in space is finished, the shuttle returns to Earth. It glides down and lands on a **runway** like an ordinary plane. Parachutes help it to slow down.

Timeline

1783 A hot-air balloon made by the Montgolfier brothers in France carries people into the air for the first time.

1852 The first **airship** takes off in France with its builder Henry Giffard.

1903 In the United States, the Wright brothers take off in their aeroplane *Flyer 1*. It is the first aeroplane with an **engine** to fly properly.

1933 American pilot Wiley Post flies around the world on his own. The 25,000 kilometre flight takes nearly eight days.

1969 The first Boeing 747 jumbo jet takes off for a test flight. Passengers first flew in a 747 in 1970.

1969 In France, the supersonic **airliner** Concorde flies for the first time. It starts carrying passengers in 1976.

1981 A space shuttle takes off for the first time from Kennedy Space Center in the USA. It orbits the Earth and then glides down again.

Glossary

airliner	a large plane that carries passengers
airship	a balloon with an engine to move it along
blade	one of the long, flat pieces on a propeller
cockpit	the space at the front of a plane where the pilot sits
engine	a machine that powers movement using fuel. A plane's engine moves the plane along.
goods	things that people buy and sell
hold	the part of the plane where goods and luggage are kept
jet	a type of engine. A jet engine sends out a stream of gas backwards that pushes a plane forwards.
missile	a machine that flies straight through the air and explodes when it reaches its target
nozzle	a hole where gas and hot air come out of an engine
pilot	the person who flies the plane
propeller	the part of a plane that is attached to the engine and turns to make the plane move
runway	a long, straight strip of ground where planes take off and land
steer	to guide the direction of the plane

Index